HOLT and the TEDDY BEAR

HOLT
and the
TEDDY BEAR

By Jim McCafferty

Illustrated by
Florence S. Davis

PELICAN PUBLISHING COMPANY
Gretna 2003

For Bess and Jack

First edition, 1991
First paperback edition, 1999
Second paperback printing, 2003

ISBN 1-56554-580-X

Printed in Singapore

Published by Pelican Publishing Company, Inc.
1000 Burmaster Street, Gretna, Louisiana 70053

HOLT AND THE TEDDY BEAR

Do you know how the Teddy bear got its name?

It all started a long time ago, before your mother and father were born. It was even before your grandmother and grandfather were born. Way back then there was a boy about your age named Theodore Roosevelt. That was his real name, but his friends just called him "Teddy."

Teddy lived with his mother, father, brother, and two sisters in a big house in New York City. Teddy was a smart boy. He worked hard at everything he did. Whether he was learning his lessons or swimming at the beach, he always did the very best job he could.

He especially loved the outdoors, and went camping or hiking every chance he got. As you might think, Teddy was very interested in birds and other animals. He watched them in the woods around his family's summer house, and read as many books about them as he could find. Once, he even started a museum in his bedroom. In it he had birds' nests, snake skins, pet mice, and just about everything else his mother would let him bring into the house.

Even after he grew up, Teddy still loved animals and the outdoors. When he finished college, he bought a ranch out West just so he could spend more time outside. On his ranch Teddy did all the things that the

cowboys did. He helped round up cattle, camped out under the stars, and he even hunted buffalo.

All the cowboys liked Teddy. They must have been sad when he decided to move back to New York. But the people of New York were happy, because they liked Teddy, too. They liked him so much that they elected him governor of their state.

After he became governor, more and more people got to know "Teddy" Roosevelt. And they liked him, also. It wasn't long before he became president of the United States. Then people stopped calling him "Teddy" and started calling him "Mr. Roosevelt."

But even after he became president, Mr. Roosevelt still loved the outdoors. He loved to ride horses. He loved to camp out. Most of all, he loved to hunt.

Two men in the South, Major Helm and Mr. Foote, knew how much Mr. Roosevelt liked to hunt. "Would you like to go bear hunting with us in Mississippi?" they wrote to him in a letter.

That was something Mr. Roosevelt had always wanted to do. "Yes," he wrote back to them. "I'd love to meet you in Mississippi for a bear hunt."

Major Helm and Mr. Foote were overjoyed. They began planning the hunt right away. "We must get the best hunting guide we can find for the president," Mr. Foote said. "He must be someone who knows all about the woods, and who is sure to find a bear for the president to shoot."

"Who can do that for us?" Major Helm wondered.

"Holt Collier!" both men shouted at once. "He knows more about bear hunting than anybody! We'll get Holt to be Mr. Roosevelt's guide!"

Holt Collier wasn't rich like President Roosevelt. In fact, Holt was poor. All Holt had in the whole world were his hunting dogs, his horse, his gun, and the little house he lived in. But that didn't make Holt feel sad. "I've got everything I need for hunting. And that's all I want," he would say with a smile.

When Holt was a little boy, he didn't live in a big house like Mr. Roosevelt had. He lived in a little cabin on Plum Ridge, a cotton plantation in Mississippi. Holt's parents were slaves, and his whole family worked for Mr. Howell Hinds, the man who owned the plantation. Holt's mother washed Mr. Hinds's clothes and mended his socks. Holt's father cooked Mr. Hinds's food. Even Holt and his little brother worked for Mr. Hinds. They fed his chickens and milked his cows.

But there was one way that Holt was very much like Mr. Roosevelt. He loved the outdoors. Even when he was a little boy, Holt spent as much time outside as he could. Mr. Hinds knew how much Holt liked the outdoors. Whenever he could, Mr. Hinds gave Holt chores he could do in the wide open spaces.

One day Mr. Hinds gave Holt an old shotgun and told him, "Keep the blackbirds out of the chinaberry trees in my garden with this." Holt did it, too. By the end of the day he had shot enough blackbirds for his father to make two blackbird pies. Holt gave one pie to Mr. Hinds. He and his mother, father, and brother ate the other one.

Whenever Mr. Hinds went hunting, he would let Holt ride on the horse with him. By the time Holt grew up, he could ride and shoot as well as any man in Mississippi. He also knew more about hunting bears than anybody else in the whole state. Hunters from all across the country came to Mississippi just so they could hunt with Holt Collier.

No, Holt wasn't rich like Mr. Roosevelt, but he certainly was famous. No wonder Mr. Foote and Major Helm asked him to be Mr. Roosevelt's guide.

Now, you and I might have been nervous if we had been chosen to be the guide for the president of the United States. Not Holt. "I'll find a bear for Mr. Roosevelt to shoot," he told Major Helm, "even if I have to lasso one and tie it to a tree."

"I don't think you'll have to do that," laughed Major Helm. "Mr. Roosevelt's a pretty good hunter. He shouldn't need too much help."

Holt eagerly looked forward to the day the president was to arrive. Each day he took his pack of hunting dogs to the woods to practice. "I want them to be in shape to chase bears for the president," Holt told Major Helm. While Holt followed on horseback, his hounds ran for miles and miles. All except Jocko, that is.

Jocko was a little yellow mutt that just happened to be Holt's favorite dog in the whole pack. Jocko's legs were too short for him to keep up with the other dogs, and so he was carried in a special bag hooked over Holt's saddle horn. Holt only let Jocko out of the sack and down on the ground when the other dogs had found a bear.

Jocko may have been small, but he was very brave. If a big bear caught one of the dogs and tried to hurt it, Jocko would rush in and nip the bear hard on the leg.

The bear would be so surprised that little Jocko had bitten him that he would let go of the other dog. Jocko saved the lives of many of Holt's hounds that way.

Finally the day for the president's visit arrived. Holt saddled up his horse and rode out to Major Helm's hunting camp. All of Holt's dogs followed close behind. All except Jocko, of course. He curled up in the bag on Holt's saddle and fell fast asleep.

The ride to the camp was a long one. First Holt passed through a big cotton plantation. The cotton was ready to be picked, and hung on the tall plants, white and fluffy as new snow. Then he entered the woods. The great oaks with long, gray streamers of Spanish moss hanging from them towered over Holt like huge, bearded giants. An ivory-billed woodpecker, as big as a crow, hammered away on one of the trees, "Rat-a-tat-tat! Rat-a-tat-tat!"

He sounds just like somebody playing a drum, Holt thought.

As Holt rode deeper into the forest, he began to see wild animals. A deer ran among the trees ahead of him. A family of raccoons crossed the trail in front of his horse. Overhead he heard a flock of geese, flying south for the winter.

"I could stay in these woods forever," Holt said to himself.

Soon Holt could see the white tents of the hunting camp close ahead on the banks of the Little Sunflower River. As he rode into camp, Holt saw a group of hunters gathered together. Among them were some very important men, including Mr. John M. Parker, who would later become governor of Louisiana; Mr. LeRoy Percy, who would soon become a United States senator from Mississippi; Mr. Stuyvesant Fish, who was president of one of the largest railroad companies in America; and Mr. John M. McIlhenny, whose family owned the company that makes Tabasco sauce.

In the middle of the crowd Holt spotted Major Helm and Mr. Foote. They were talking to a husky fellow wearing thick glasses, a big moustache, and a wide, friendly smile. That must be President Roosevelt, Holt decided. He climbed down from his horse and let Jocko out of the saddlebag. Then he walked toward Major Helm. "Mr. Roosevelt," Major Helm said, "I want you to meet Holt Collier. He'll be your guide on this hunt."

"That's right, Mr. President," said Holt, "and my dog Jocko and I are going to get you a bear to shoot, even if we have to lasso one and tie it to a tree."

"Err-ruff! Ruff!" barked Jocko, as if to agree with Holt.

"Bully!" said Mr. Roosevelt. "And bully for you, too, Jocko!" That was his way of saying, "Well, that's fine and dandy with me!"

Mr. Roosevelt loved the hunting camp. It was way out in the woods, many miles from the nearest town. There were no electric lights and no bathtubs. There were just tents, horses, and hunting dogs. "It reminds me of when I worked on my ranch out West," he told Holt. "Those were some of the happiest days of my life."

The first night in camp, the men built a big fire and cooked supper on it. After everyone had eaten, they sat around the glowing red coals and talked.

"Tell us a story, Holt," said the president. Holt did just that, and what a storyteller he was! He told hunting tales about all the big bears and panthers he had seen. He talked about his adventures in the army during the Civil War. He even talked about the time he had helped capture a gang of outlaws on an island in the Mississippi River.

"Bully!" cried President Roosevelt at the end of every story. "I could listen to you all night, Holt."

"We'd better not do that, Mr. Roosevelt," said Major Helm. "Tomorrow we're going bear hunting. We need our rest."

"That's right," agreed Holt.

"Well, I suppose," said Mr. Roosevelt reluctantly.

The president, Major Helm, Mr. Foote, and Holt all went to their tents, blew out their lanterns, and fell asleep. Everything was still and peaceful. Except for Jocko. He lay by the fireside, kicking and barking in his sleep, dreaming he was chasing the biggest bear in the woods.

It was still dark when Holt woke up the next morning. All the woods were quiet. The only sound was the lonely hooting of an owl somewhere far off in the swamps. "Who, who, who-ooh. Who, who, who-oooooh!"

This is my favorite time of day, Holt thought as he listened to the owl.

Holt went straight to work getting everything ready for the hunt. First he lit a fire. "I want the president to be warm when he wakes up," he said to himself. Then he woke the cooks and asked them to start breakfast. "Make plenty of food," he told them. "The president likes to eat."

Next he saddled his horse and rounded up all the hunting dogs. "Wake up, sleepyhead," he said to Jocko. "You can't lie around dreaming all day."

Jocko barked a greeting to Holt. "And be quiet," Holt whispered to his dog. "There are some people in this camp who like to sleep even more than you do."

After everything was just right, Holt went to wake the president. But Mr. Roosevelt was already awake. "I got up about the same time you did, Holt," said Mr. Roosevelt. "I've been in my tent writing letters to my two girls and four boys back home. They will want to hear all about you and Jocko. But right now, Holt, I can smell bacon frying. Let's eat breakfast."

The cooks had done more than just fry bacon. They brought out platter after platter piled with sausage, eggs, ham, biscuits, and pancakes. Mr. Roosevelt watched as the cooks placed the food on the camp table. "Bully!" said Mr. Roosevelt. "I don't get food this good at the White House. I think I'll have a little bit of everything, Holt. Or maybe a lot of everything!"

After breakfast, Major Helm blew a long note on his hunting horn. "Mount up," he said. "Let the bear hunt begin!" Holt, the president, and the other men swung up into their saddles.

"Come with me, Mr. Roosevelt," Holt said. And so the president and Holt rode off into the woods, surrounded by Holt's hunting dogs. Some of the hounds were out front and some were behind. Some were on the right and some were on the left. But all had their noses to the ground, sniffing for the smell of bear. All except for Jocko, of course. He stayed in his special bag, hanging from Holt's saddle.

The woods were beautiful that November morning. The leaves had turned from their summer green to their fall colors of gold, orange, red, and yellow. An icy frost sparkled on the grass like diamond dust. "It's a

bully day for a bear hunt, isn't it, Holt?" said the president.

Before Holt could answer, one of the hounds began to make a barking, howling sound that hunters call "baying."

"When old Remus bays like that," Holt told Mr. Roosevelt, "it means he smells a bear trail."

"Bully!" replied the president.

Soon all the dogs began to bay. Then they started running faster and faster. "They've got one for sure, Mr. Roosevelt," Holt said.

"Giddyup," Holt said to his horse. "Follow those dogs."

"Giddyup," said Mr. Roosevelt, and soon he and Holt were racing through the thick forest.

It wasn't easy keeping up with the hounds. The woods were almost like a jungle, and the branches beat against Holt and the president as their horses galloped through the trees. Briers tore their clothes. Sometimes the thick tangles of vines almost pulled them from their saddles as they rushed along. Once the woods got so thick that Holt had to stop and cut vines away with his knife before the horses could go any farther.

But soon they came to a clearing and the riding became easier. Then they saw it! A big, fat black bear, half running, half waddling across a cornfield next to a farmhouse. The dogs were not far behind.

Holt and the president rode faster, trying to catch up with the hounds and the bear. Just as they reached the middle of the field, a farmer came running out of the house. "Get out of my cornfield!" he yelled. "Get off my land!"

Holt stopped his horse. "Don't you know who you're talking to?" he asked the farmer. "This is Mr. Theodore Roosevelt, the president of the United States."

The farmer suddenly looked afraid. But before he could say anything, Mr. Roosevelt said, "He's right, Holt. This is his land. Bear or no bear, even the president doesn't have the right to come riding across it without asking him first. We'll go back the way we came."

By the time Holt and the president found the dogs again, the bear had gotten away. The president, Holt, the horses, and the dogs hunted the rest of the morning without finding another sign of him.

"It looks like we've lost him, Holt," said Mr. Roosevelt.

"Don't worry, Mr. President," Holt said. "Like I told you, I'll find you a bear to shoot, even if I have to lasso one and tie it to a tree."

But they hunted for another two hours and there was still no bear to be found. The horses were tired. The dogs were tired. All the men from the hunting camp were tired. But Holt and the president kept on hunting.

By the middle of the afternoon, Holt began to worry. I told the president I'd find him a bear, he thought, and I'm going to do it, one way or another.

He took the president to every place in the woods where he had ever seen a bear before. But still they could not find a bear. He took the dogs to every trail where they had ever smelled a bear before. But they still had no luck. "It's getting late," said the president. "We'd better go back to camp before the others start looking for us."

"You go on back," Holt told Mr. Roosevelt. "I'm going to hunt for just a few minutes longer."

As he rode away from Mr. Roosevelt, Holt heard his dogs baying in the distance. They must have found the trail of a bear, Holt thought. But a trail alone was not good enough for him and the president. Holt wanted to find the bear that had made it.

Where could that bear have gone on a day like today? he wondered.

Although it was November, the sun was shining

brightly that afternoon. The air was dry. Holt was hot and thirsty, and he reached for his canteen to get a drink of water. He let the cool water run down his throat. "That's it!" he shouted aloud. "If I'm hot and thirsty, the bears must be, too!"

He rode as fast as he could to the old water hole on Coon Bayou. He rode so fast, in fact, that his dogs couldn't keep up with him. He rode so fast that Jocko nearly fell out of his saddlebag.

When Holt reached Coon Bayou, he saw just what he had thought he would see: a hot, tired old bear drinking his fill of water.

Jocko saw the bear, too. He leapt from the saddle-bag and hit the ground barking. The noise scared the bear, and he waded out a few feet into the water.

Without the other dogs here, Holt thought, Jocko could get hurt. I'd better stop him before he gets too close to that bear.

"Wait, Jocko!" Holt called. But it was too late. Jocko

was already charging into the bayou, barking with all his might. The bear showed his teeth and growled. But that didn't stop Jocko. The bear reared up onto his hind legs, towering over the little dog. Jocko moved in even closer. Without warning, the bear suddenly swung his paw toward Jocko. But Jocko was too quick for him. He jumped out of the way just in time to keep from being slashed by the bear's sharp claws.

That just made the bear more angry. He snapped his huge teeth and made another grab for Jocko. This time, Jocko was in deeper water, and couldn't move fast enough. The huge bear had the little dog between his big arms.

Holt sprang off his horse and ran toward the bear. "Let go of my dog!" he shouted. "Let go of my dog!" Holt raised his gun and aimed at the bear. But he didn't pull the trigger. I might hit Jocko, he thought.

Instead, Holt ran a few steps into the water toward the bear. Swinging the gun like a club, Holt hit the bear on the head with all his strength. The bear dropped Jocko and fell over into the shallow edge of the bayou, knocked out cold.

After two or three minutes had passed, the old bear began to wake up and to try to get back on his feet. As Holt watched him, he remembered what he had told the president. "I'll get you a bear to shoot," he had said, "even if I have to lasso one and tie it to a tree."

Holt ran back to his horse and got the rope that was tied to his saddle horn. He made a lasso noose and twirled it above his head the way he had learned to in the army. He let the lasso fly, and it landed right around the old bear's head.

Holt climbed back onto his horse and tied the end of the rope to his saddle horn. "Giddyup," he told his horse. The horse backed up slowly, pulling the bear out of the water and onto dry land. Jocko, who thought he had won the fight all by himself, led the way, barking with pride.

Holt stopped his horse and tied the bear to a tree. The old bear seemed very tired now, and Holt began to feel sorry for him. "But I can't let him go," Holt said to himself. "I promised the president a bear."

Holt put his hunting horn to his lips and blew it three times as a signal for all the others to come and find him. "Bah-umph! Bah-umph! Bah-umph!"

Some of the men in camp rushed out to see why Holt was calling them. All the dogs from the camp came out, too. When they saw the bear, they began to bark and snap at him, but the bear just sat there and took it. He was too tired to fight back.

When the bear caught Jocko in the bayou, Holt thought, he looked mighty big and mean. But now that he's tied up and surrounded by all these dogs and people, he doesn't seem big and mean at all.

More than ever, Holt wanted to let the bear go.

Then up walked Mr. Roosevelt. Nobody ever looked more surprised than the president did when he saw that old bear tied to the tree.

"Well, Holt," he said, "you told me you'd get a bear for me, and you did it."

"Shoot the bear, Mr. President," someone yelled from the back of the crowd.

"Don't shoot him," Holt whispered to Mr. Roosevelt. "Let him go."

"Yeah," somebody else shouted. "Shoot it. That's what you came here for."

"Don't shoot him, Mr. President," Holt murmured quietly.

"Don't worry, Holt," the president whispered back, "I don't intend to."

"Well," somebody else said, "are you going to shoot it or not?"

"No!" Mr. Roosevelt shouted back to the crowd. "I've hunted game all over America and I'm proud to be a hunter. But I couldn't be proud of myself if I shot an old, tired, worn-out bear that was tied to a tree."

"Bully!" said Holt.

There was a newspaper reporter among the hunters that day and he wrote a story about Mr. Roosevelt and the bear. A man who drew cartoons read the reporter's newspaper story. He liked the story so much that he drew a picture of Mr. Roosevelt and the bear. A toymaker saw the picture. He liked the picture so much that he began making stuffed toy animals which he called "Teddy bears," in honor of Mr. Roosevelt.

Soon, the little stuffed bears were just about the most popular toys in the world. And as you know, they still are, and boys and girls everywhere still call them Teddy bears.

That's how Holt and the president gave the Teddy bear its name.

And that's a bully story, don't you think?

Epilogue

Holt Collier hunted bear with President Roosevelt once more in 1907 in Louisiana, and Mr. Roosevelt kept in touch with Holt until the president's death in 1919. Holt Collier died over twenty-seven years later on August 1, 1936. He was ninety years old. There is a street named in his honor in Greenville, Mississippi.

Mr. Foote's grandson, born years after the hunt, grew up to become the well-known writer and historian, Shelby Foote. Mr. LeRoy Percy, besides becoming famous in his own right as a senator, had a very famous great-nephew, novelist Walker Percy. And of course, John McIlhenny's family, of New Iberia, Louisiana, continues to make their famous Tabasco sauce.

Mr. Morris Michtom, the toymaker who first named the Teddy bear, went on to found the Ideal toy company.

The only surviving building connected in any way with Holt Collier and Teddy Roosevelt's famous bear hunt is Mount Holly, a beautiful brick Italianate mansion situated on the shores of Lake Washington, just south of Greenville, Mississippi. Once the home of Mr. Foote, the bear hunter, today it serves as a private home and a bed & breakfast inn.